Paramount Market Publishing, Inc.
950 Danby Road, Suite 136
Ithaca, NY 14850
www.paramountbooks.com
Voice: 607-275-8100; 888-787-8100 Fax: 607-275-8101

Publisher: James Madden
Editorial Director: Doris Walsh

ISBN 13: 978-1-941688-29-8 | ISBN 10: 1-941688-29-2
Printed in the United States of America

I F**KING LOVE THAT COMPANY

How a New Generation of Brand Builders Is Defining the Post-Amazon World

Written by Bayard Winthrop & Randy Komisar

GONE

BUST

RISE

GO

DEATH BY A THOUSAND CUTS

Blockbuster as we knew it folded last year— finally. For the onetime video rental giant, it was an ugly, drawn-out demise that surprised no one in the end. For years, customers had signaled their unwillingness to subsidize the enormous expenses of the video rental chain whose bright blue-and-gold logo shone like a beacon in malls and shopping districts nationwide.

Today, Blockbuster has come to symbolize the dark side of disruption—a hackneyed buzzword describing the sea change that occurs in an industry when technology essentially enables a company to build a better mousetrap. Like Tower Records and Borders before it, Blockbuster saw its differentiation collapse into irrelevance in the new digital world of purchasing and streaming downloadable media.

Now the digital world's disruption has set its sights on a new set of victims. Instead of purveyors of movies, music, and books, the latest casualties range from clothing companies to coffee shops to electronics stores. Go to any mall and you'll see the signs: too few shoppers and too many sales signs promoting low-quality, ho-hum selections of apparel, accessories, and whatever else can be shoved into a square box of space. The seismic economic shifts associated with electronic distribution and social marketing are rendering businesses built on physical real estate obsolete.

We are living in an Amazon world. It is a world defined by automation, where giants like Walmart and Amazon leverage technology to make the entire process of finding, buying, and delivering products easier, cheaper, and more efficient. Amazon.com has single-handedly created its own category of retail: big box e-tail. We flock to Amazon to stock up on socks, shampoo, and other essentials that meet a minimum threshold of quality but whose real draw is their low prices and prompt delivery. We love Amazon for its clinical efficiency.

Amazon is at the forefront of a continuum of advances that have changed the face of retail. The introduction of the Sears Roebuck print catalog in the 1890s was a huge technological feat that gave settlers in the West access to goods they couldn't find nearby. As towns grew, so did Main Street and the brick-and-mortar stores that populated it. Eventually these shops were driven out of business, first by national department stores and then by Walmart. Online distribution and online sales were the next stage in technology's drive to make retail more efficient and automated. Today, Amazon embodies the latest iteration of a revolution that has been more than a 100 years in the making.

The rise of online distribution and sales, combined with the power of social media, is beginning to unseat several generations of brands built on brick-and-mortar dynamics. Specialty apparel brands such as Quiksilver, American Apparel, Abercrombie & Fitch, Aeropostale, and Wet Seal are suffering the same slow suffocation that brought down Blockbuster. Even older brands such as Gap and Banana Republic face bleak futures. Classic department stores such as Macy's, JCPenney, and Sears, too, grapple with the harsh reality that shopping behaviors are changing in ways that seriously devalue what they have to offer.[1] Among electronics stores, RadioShack's death spiral has been excruciating to watch. The takeaway: in today's retail market, *any* business that relies on physical foot traffic for sales risks going under. As Warren Buffett warned Berkshire Hathaway investors earlier this year, retail "in particular is facing major threats."[2]

A Revolutionary Blueprint for Retail

For all the pain brick-and-mortar stores are experiencing, the future of brand building is filled with opportunity. Today we are living in an Amazon world, but tomorrow's universe will

ANNUAL REVENUE OF SELECT APPAREL COMPANIES

As revenue flattens, retailers are forced into a series of bad choices to try to recover top-line growth.

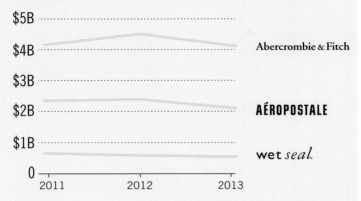

MARKET CAPITALIZATION OF SELECT DEPARTMENT STORES

As customers move online, the capital markets punish traditional retailers.

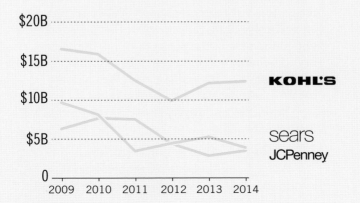

Source: S&P CapitalIQ

look and operate differently. We're seeing the rise of two distinct types of brands, both enabled by technology. The first group is the *automators*. These brands will continue to do what Sears Roebuck, Walmart, and Amazon did: they will leverage the latest technology to make finding, buying, and delivering products at the lowest prices possible even easier. Amazon will continue to dominate this category of commerce, but new brands built on an entirely different model are emerging from its shadow as online sales figures in the United States continue to grow by double digits every year.[3]

These nascent brands do more than automate customer interactions—they humanize them. In between the rise of Amazon and the death of brick and mortar, a huge white space has developed in the retail experience. Filling that space are young brands whose primary goal is to give consumers something they can care about, beyond basic necessities like socks and shampoo. These brands build an emotional connection with consumers and provide a personalized experience the way mom-and-pop shops did in a previous era. Instead of hanging up a shingle on Main Street, however, these *humanizers* leverage the Web and social media to create direct, personal relationships on a massive scale. These brands both fill and understand the white space in retail. In the end, brand building will bifurcate into two camps: the automators and the humanizers. We call this the post-Amazon world.

Three key catalysts are driving the transformation of brands:

- **Access is virtually universal.** Brands throughout history have differentiated themselves by getting as physically close as possible to consumers. With technology, that access is now ubiquitous.

- **Business models built on brick-and-mortar stores and layers of distribution are suffocating under their own weight.** Most retailers today are little more than real estate developers. The costs necessary to support vast infrastructures built on leases and global supply chains have become serious liabilities.

- **Customers actively build and shape brands via social media.** We titled this book *I F**king Love That Company* for a reason. Today, when customers feel loyal to a brand, they let the world know about it—and don't hold back. Companies that are unable to inspire love and loyalty will die.

The new breed of brands operates according to a fresh set of rules and expectations. Size, scale, and speed don't define success for them. Efficiency, quality, company values—and the power of an Instagram plug—do. For these companies, the Internet is their storefront; a physical presence provides nothing more than an opportunity to connect with customers, not to push product. Growth alone isn't the endgame; scaling to meet customer demand is. Above all, these upstarts prize the human touch—albeit with no physical presence—in every customer interaction and in all aspects of their business.

We have already seen numerous young companies embrace this new model and thrive. Warby Parker. Nasty Gal. American Giant. Lolly Wolly Doodle. The list goes on. We don't know which ones will become household names and which ones will remain niche players, but this much we do know: everything we've come to expect about brand building in the past century is changing—and fast. ■

BU

ST
⚠

THE FALL OF BRICK-AND-MORTAR BRANDS

The history of brand building—capitalism,
really—has long been punctuated by moments of
severe disruption followed by extended periods
of sustained calm. To understand what's happening
to brands today, it's important to understand how
disruption has made an impact on the customer
relationship almost from the start.

For hundreds of years, the "retail" model
centered on individuals who specialized in making
products or providing services in which they had
expertise. Some made clothes or sold furniture,
others baked bread or farmed crops. Everyone
survived by specializing in something he or she
did well and then using the profits to buy products
and services from other specialists. Choices were
limited, but for consumers, the whole experience
was profoundly personal.

The game changed when distribution became
the primary driver for brands. Sears Roebuck
used the technology tools at its disposal to print and
deliver catalogs to rural homesteaders. The Main
Street stores that eventually sprang up to serve
these new communities were replaced by department stores such as JCPenney. By the middle of the
20th century, the mall era was born. Vast shopping
complexes populated with large department stores
and smaller specialty shops came to define the
American shopping experience.

In the wave of disruption that followed,
Walmart symbolized scale and low cost. The
company's strategy wasn't rocket science; it merely
converted all those Sears catalogs into actual
storefronts as a way of bringing consumers ever
closer to a wide array of goods. Just as Walmart
pushed out the local five-and-dime, Zales wiped
out the family jeweler, and Dick's Sporting Goods
put the neighborhood sports shop out of business.
Barnes & Noble cornered books and Tower
Records took music. Eventually, iconic manufac-
turers got into the game: Levi's and others like it

pursued access and choice by pushing more doors out into suburbia in a race for scale.

The High Price of Scale at the Mall

The suburban mall was an amazing innovation. It epitomized the Amazon of its time, delivering unprecedented access and convenience. It brought consumers together in beautiful structures filled with an incredible assortment of products and beloved brands. The anchor tenants were often Sears or JCPenney, giant department stores with seemingly endless inventory and specialty sections for items like books, lingerie, or shoes. Smaller vendors jockeyed to be near the department stores, because the proximity brought foot traffic to their niche businesses. Malls became the ticket to building scale for brands. A mall vendor could open a new store and watch the revenue pour in. More stores led to more foot traffic. More foot traffic drove sales, and businesses thrived. Scale became the true north for specialty brands and department stores alike. Powered by massive marketing budgets, malls became a substantive part of our culture. They offered not only access and assortment but also a social hub for gathering with friends and family.

Malls created inestimable value for consumers and brands. Even though the mall model came at a steep price for the brands, which became developers of vast portfolios of real estate, that wasn't a problem. Until the Web came along.

With the Internet, "real estate" suddenly became infinite, cheap, and always open. The arrival of e-commerce two decades ago marked the beginning of the slow, steady decline of the local mall. The once-savvy bet that mall occupants made on physical real estate has turned sour. Seeking scale in the face of the new threat of online commerce, brands and retailers have been forced to make cuts that, in the end, have hurt customers. Customer service has

AMERICAN APPAREL, ABERCROMBIE & FITCH STOCK PRICE PERFORMANCE

Traditional retailers that are unable to combat the macro trends of declining foot traffic are unable to maintain compelling value propositions, setting off a domino effect of bad decisions and declining market capitalization.

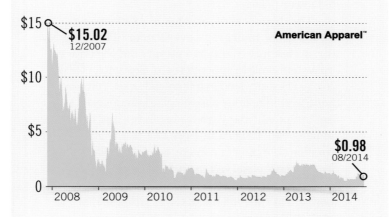

American Apparel™

$15.02
12/2007

$0.98
08/2014

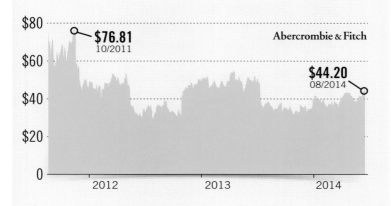

Abercrombie & Fitch

$76.81
10/2011

$44.20
08/2014

declined. Brands have sacrificed the values that long defined their success. Product quality, for example, has suffered as brands have moved manufacturing offshore in the hunt for ever-cheaper labor.

Today, the relationship between mall retailers and consumers is frayed. Although some mall vendors revel in periods of hyper growth, overall the bonds between brick-and-mortar brands and consumers grow weaker. E-commerce has accelerated this deterioration by building new relationships built on convenience, massive assortment, and lower prices.

The drumbeat of grim news about smaller crowds at the mall grows ever louder.[4] This upheaval worries not just traditional players but the entire ecosystem built to support them. Starbucks CEO Howard Schultz said in a financial press release that the 2013 holiday shopping season marked the first time that "many traditional brick and mortar retailers experienced in-store foot traffic give way to online shopping in a major way."[5] As *Bloomberg Businessweek* observed the next day, Schultz might be getting nervous for one simple reason: fewer shoppers at the mall mean fewer lattes sold at the nearest Starbucks.[6]

Storm Clouds on the Horizon

In the battle for e-commerce dollars, mall retailers made a crucial mistake: they brought knives to a gunfight. Sure, they built shiny websites with online catalogs that mirrored their offline selections. They grew savvy about email marketing and offers of free shipping. But none of this came at the expense of their commitment to offline growth. Some retailers, such as Circuit City, continued to open new stores and were crushed by Amazon's leaner model. Others, such Best Buy, PetSmart, and RadioShack, have managed to hang on even as they struggle to define new value propositions for their customers.[7]

To understand why so many old-world brands

E-COMMERCE VS. TRADITIONAL RETAIL GROWTH IN APPAREL

E-commerce sales grow strongly while traditional retail is barely keeping up with inflation.

Average Annual Sales Growth, 2008–2012

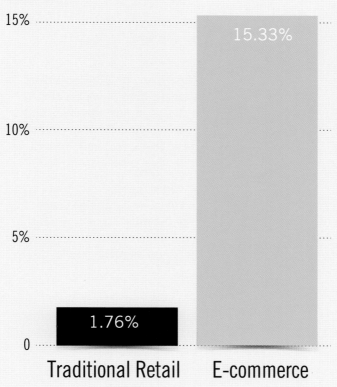

15%

15.33%

10%

5%

1.76%

0

Traditional Retail   **E-commerce**

Source: U.S. Census Bureau, Annual Retail Trade Survey, 2013

will inevitably fail, let's take a closer look at what has become, for many of them, their albatross:

- **Supply chains.** The many layers that exist between the sourcing of raw materials and putting a finished product onto store shelves are enormously expensive and difficult to manage. Global supply chains force retailers to gamble on inventory far in advance and to spend too much time and money overseeing the entire process.

- **Real estate.** Old-world retailers have little choice but to double as real estate developers and managers. Sales per square foot now trumps customer loyalty as a measure of success.

- **Inventory.** Because many brands depend on hundreds of physical outlets, each location must represent all the products that a brand sells. This approach requires large inventory bets (lots of cash up front) and massive write-downs (discounts) when those bets go bad.

- **Marketing.** To keep stores full requires expensive national and local ad campaigns exhorting consumers to buy the must-have items of the season. The top 25 largest retail advertisers alone spent $7.9 billion on media marketing in 2012.[8]

How do retailers pay for all of this? They focus on driving extremely high initial product margins (translation: they try to get customers to foot the bill at checkout). For a brick-and-mortar retailer to have any hope of succeeding, the initial price of a newly-arrived cashmere coat, for example, must drastically exceed the cost of manufacturing it. Retailers bet that high margins will drive gross profit to pay for all the marketing and distribution that went into making those winter coats and attracting

THE DEATH SPIRAL
OF BAD CHOICES

As investors demand increasing market cap,
management is forced to try to reengineer growth.
All the choices available are bad and often end up eating
whatever muscle is left in the business.

CHOICE 1
**SHUT DOWN
STORES**

CHOICE 2
**REDUCE
MARKETING
BUDGET**

REDUCE ACCESS

REDUCE SALE

REDUCE SALE

REDUCE QUALITY

DEATH

REDUCE INTEREST

CHOICE 4
**MAKE
CHEAPER
PRODUCTS**

REDUCE SALE

REDUCE SALE

REDUCE INTER-ACTION

CHOICE 3
**REDUCE
STAFF**

buyers, with enough left over for a small profit. This explains why net profit margins in the retail industry, spanning everything from groceries to electronics to apparel, average just 4 percent.[9]

Razor-thin profit margins don't leave a lot of room for error—and that is the fundamental flaw in the old-world model. Flat or declining sales can put a retailer out of business almost overnight. To stay afloat, retailers face only bad choices: they can close stores, lay off employees, take fewer inventory positions, or spend less on advertising. Each scenario involves painful, but necessary, trade-offs. Slash marketing budgets, for instance, and a key tool for luring shoppers into physical stores evaporates. Reduce the number of sales reps on the floor and customer service declines. These measures, aimed at shoring up brand finances in the short run, usually hurt customer loyalty in the long run.

Without consistent top-line growth, these businesses, under pressure to recover growth, become financially unstable and die. Already we're seeing hallmarks of the mall era—Best Buy, JCPenney, Abercrombie & Fitch, American Apparel, and Sears, to name just a few—being crushed under the weight of costs to support aspects of their business that no longer resonate with consumers. Sales at the average JCPenney nosedived 30 percent from 2011 through earlier this year.[10] Coldwater Creek, Staples, GameStop, and The Children's Place are closing stores.[11] American Apparel shares, which once traded at around $15 apiece, hovered around $1 for most of 2014. Abercrombie shares, once valued at more than $75 each, fetch less than $40.

Disruption's New Dawn

When someone builds a better mousetrap, the unraveling of the status quo usually follows. That phenomenon isn't new in the history of business, and it's not new in the history of brand building. Blockbuster, Borders, and Tower Records went out of business because Amazon came along and improved the overall customer experience by eliminating unnecessary layers of cost and by delivering better, less expensive products more conveniently. That same vacuuming out of excess costs is now disrupting all retail.

None of this shift would have been possible without technology. Today, we're seeing digital technology's impact deepen as a new wave of pure-play e-commerce businesses leverages the operational efficiencies that Amazon perfected to build a different kind of retailer. These aren't wannabe Amazons whose sole mission is to provide customers with a first-rate experience when shopping for school supplies. These companies stand for more than convenience and low cost; they seek to create products and services that customers truly love. In this new paradigm, scale and personalization happily coexist.

The speed at which e-commerce brands are rewriting the rules of brand building is astounding— and accelerating as traditional retailers struggle. A whole new generation of brands is rising up, unencumbered by inefficient and burdensome distribution channels, inventory bets, and marketing campaigns. These brands happily cede the market for commodity products to Amazon. For them, the opportunity lies in goods that consumers identify with personally and feel passionate about. Maybe their passion is sports or sewing. Maybe it's designer clothes. Whatever the hobby or interest may be, post-Amazon brands offer products that customers truly love and a level of service that has been missing online and off.

Ironically, this new breed is emerging at a time when consumers are putting a premium on the very things that so many incumbent brands have been willing to sacrifice in the name of cost control: exceptional products, strong brand values, and outstanding quality. ■

RI

SE

☼
↑

THE RISE OF A(NOTHER) NEW BRAND OF RETAILER

Consumers today want more. They love
Amazon's laserlike focus on price, access, and
convenience. But consumers yearn for the intimacy
and craftsmanship they once knew from the Main
Street merchant. This desire is vividly clear in
the wild growth of farmers' markets, artisanal
craft makers, and microbreweries, among other
businesses reminiscent of the mom-and-pop shops
of yore.

But can you translate this relatively local-
ized experience into something broader and more
accessible to the masses? Can the idea of artisanal
quality and personal connections exist beyond
the bounds of a neighborhood farmers' market?
And can it exist with prices that the mainstream
consumer can afford?

The answers are yes, yes, and yes. Technology
not only makes possible lower prices, unlimited
inventory, and lightning-fast transactions, it also
opens up a host of new opportunities in the realms
of quality, intimacy, and accessibility. Three factors
fuel this revolution:

- **Social wildfire.** Social media isn't a pass-
  ing trend, but a permanent change affecting
  everything consumers and brands do. Social
  media is marketing, product innovation, and
  customer service rolled into one. It supersedes
  all previous metrics for building brands and
  represents the most powerful technology shift
  in just about every industry. It makes marketing less expensive. It speeds brand building. It
  drives product development and selection.

- **Mobile technology's rise.** Mobile speeds up
  everything. It's not merely a channel to the
  consumer; it *is* the consumer. Mobile technology makes social media fluid and accelerates
  brand building.

- **Big data.** It's the story of our time: more
  than ever, we have huge amounts of data

about what people want and need today, and what they will want and need tomorrow. Data analytics drives better customer experiences across industries as companies discover unprecedented levels of insight into consumers and their behaviors.

Technology has leveled the distribution playing field. Every online vendor can offer convenience, service, and choice to customers. What sets today's emerging retailers apart—and gives them a distinct competitive advantage—is the ability to know their customers better and to serve them better than other retailers, including the automators.

How is this possible? Because brands today can start fresh, unencumbered by the costs of complex distribution channels, massive marketing budgets, and huge inventory bets. They exist almost exclusively online (the exception being when they open a pop-up store in SoHo or some other trendy shopping district to draw attention), which enables them to deploy costs into things customers truly care about. Big box e-tailers, including Amazon, while freed from distribution costs, still act as a store and are still beholden to margins of the brands they sell. New brands start without those margins, without marketing costs, and without stores, so savings can be reinvested into higher quality products, better service, and stronger brand values.

Young brands today have choices that old-world brands and big box e-tailers don't. And if they execute well, these new brands can unlock the most powerful marketing channel in the history of the world: social networks. A business that successfully taps into its customers' passion for its products can grow quickly without the massive capital outlays required of traditional brands.

LIBERATED COSTS FREE UP INVESTMENT OPPORTUNITIES

Unshackled from old-world costs, the new brands are able to invest in things that matter to customers, such as lower cost, better quality, and sturdier brand values

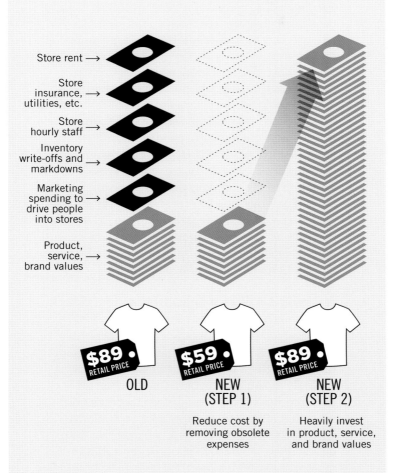

Store rent →

Store insurance, utilities, etc. →

Store hourly staff →

Inventory write-offs and markdowns →

Marketing spending to drive people into stores →

Product, service, brand values →

$89 RETAIL PRICE

$59 RETAIL PRICE

$89 RETAIL PRICE

OLD

NEW (STEP 1)

NEW (STEP 2)

Reduce cost by removing obsolete expenses

Heavily invest in product, service, and brand values

A Seamstress, an Idea, and Social Media

Consider Lolly Wolly Doodle. The online children's clothing store was founded by a North Carolina mom who used the leftover fabric from hand-sewn dresses for her daughter to launch a multimillion-dollar brand that functions exclusively online.

The secret to Lolly Wolly Doodle's success? Facebook. The company makes prototype clothing designs and showcases them on the social media site to gauge customer interest. The most popular ones get made and sold through LollyWollyDoodle.com, where girls' dresses can be had for $29. Today, less than five years after launching, Lolly Wolly Doodle boasts nearly 1 million Facebook fans (nearly twice the audience size of OshKosh B'Gosh, the 120-year-old maker of children's clothes). As sales soar at Lolly Wolly Doodle, top global brands and venture capital firms are paying very close attention to the company and its playbook.[12]

Lolly Wolly Doodle is reinventing the supply chain in retail, much as Dell did in the PC industry 20 years ago. And the company is thriving, because it gives consumers something in which to believe and participate—at an affordable price.

A Closer Look at a Brand-New Cost Stack

Traditional retailers don't have the luxury of this level of customer input or inventory control. They're stuck with an antiquated business model that forces them to cut costs where they can—typically during production. Cheap labor, for example, has become one of the most common ways that old-world retailers seek to minimize costs. The strategy carries enormous risk. Gap, for instance, announced plans in June 2014 to manufacture in Myanmar, becoming the first major US retailer to do so.[13] Despite the country's political instability, lack of infrastructure, and poor human rights record, the promise of low wages has proven irresistible to the company.

Young brands today have choices that old-world brands and big box e-tailers don't. And if they execute well, these new brands can unlock the most powerful marketing channel in the history of the world: social networks. A business that successfully taps into its customers' passion for its products can grow quickly without the massive capital outlays required of traditional brands.

The obsession with cost-cutting forces companies like Gap to make a Hobson's choice: They can try to find ways to capture and hold onto the brand love that is so vital in today's marketplace. Or they can try to go toe-to-toe

GREAT MOMENTS IN RETAIL

The key moments that drove change and improved customer satisfaction in retail.

1850s

CORNER MARKET

Based mainly in East Coast cities (model gradually spreads west with settlement), the market is a place to sell fish, groceries, and nonfood staples. For apparel, this includes the tailor. All of these businesses are independently owned.

1950s

MALL

Malls offer an efficient and accessible venue to bring together specialty shops and large department stores like "anchors" Sears and Macy's. Although they offer assortment and a social component, malls offer little or no personalization and emotional connection.

1970s

BIG BOX RETAIL

Cheap and scale become the mantra for big box retailers. For these enormous, impersonal stores, it's all about price and assortment, less about experience, and not at all about emotional connection, or love.

with Amazon and the handful of brands that have brilliantly struck a balance between access, convenience, and cost on one hand and quality on the other—brands such as Japanese apparel maker Uniqlo and Spanish clothier Zara.[14] The first

1890s

CATALOG

The Sears Roebuck catalog emerges because people are moving west and don't have access to corner markets. (This catalog was the Amazon of its time.)

1920s

MAIN STREET

Mom-and-pop shops spring up in downtowns across the country. As cars become popular, town develop. Main street shops offer highly personalized experience. Shopkeepers know customers by name and build relationships with them.

2000s

BIG BOX E-TAIL

When "big box" moves online, e-tailers see massive efficiency. Customers see endless assortment and super convenience; they feel connection to an easy process but nothing like deep love for a brand they care about.

2010s

POST-AMAZON

E-tail gets personal, offering customers all the benefits of big box e-tail plus lots of love. Customers reap emotional connection to new brands and receive personalized attention.

choice becomes increasingly unworkable when cost-cutting degrades product quality and the overall customer experience. The second choice creates a commodity business in a space already dominated by supremely efficient players.

Front-Runners in Retail's New World

Amazon tackled the problem of distribution and did it extraordinarily well. Now, a new generation of brands is filling a void in retail and taking the idea of direct-to-consumer commerce and brand building to another level. Empowered by more dynamic cost structures, these brands focus on specific product categories, often control manufacturing from start to finish, create unbelievable customer experiences, and invite consumers to participate in shaping the business.

Here are some examples of post-Amazon brands that boast a focus on delivering more to consumers:

- **Value: Warby Parker** has emerged as one of retail's fastest-growing brands. Dubbed the "Netflix of eyewear" by *GQ* magazine, Warby Parker is giving LensCrafters a run for its money.[15] American Express and Mickey Drexler (who is best known for his success at Gap and J. Crew) are among the investors betting that Warby Parker's strategy of making its own products and selling them directly to consumers at much lower prices represents the future of eyewear sales.

- **Assortment:** Identified as the fastest growing private retailer in 2012 by *Inc. Magazine*,[16] **Nasty Gal** sells apparel for young women exclusively online. In its fierce competition with Aeropostale and Wet Seal, the e-tailer has succeeded by allocating extra dollars to ensuring that it can move quickly to curate extensive, unique collections that appeal to customers who care deeply about the latest fashion trends.

- **Experience: True & Co.** is reimagining the way lingerie is designed, engineered, shopped for and lived in. The San Francisco-based brand is helping women to understand what flatters their specific shape. True & Co. delivers perfectly fit bras using a fit quiz and eliminating fitting rooms, measuring tapes and photos. The net result is a completely new experience for women.

- **Quality:** San Francisco–based **American Giant** wasn't even a year old when *Slate* declared the company's signature sweatshirt the "Greatest Hoodie Ever Made."[17] Sales grew tenfold the following year. With commitments to using only the highest quality cotton and to manufacturing in the United States, the company still struggles to keep up with demand for its $89 zip-up hoodie, which is available only online.

These companies offer more than a shopping destination. They've created, at breathtaking speeds, the kinds of long-lasting customer relationships that define great brands. We don't know yet which brands will ultimately define retail's future, but together they are building the template for the ones that will. ■

LO

VE

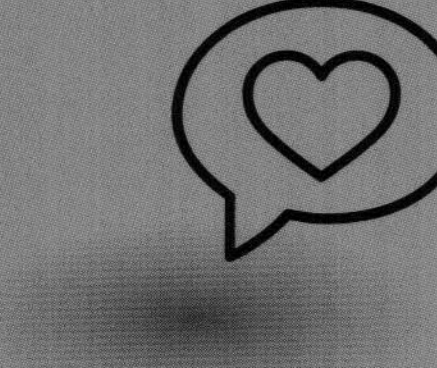

THE EMPOWERED CONSUMER

How often do we hear comments along the lines of "Remember how good Levi's jeans used to be?" or "Grandma's old KitchenAid mixer still works like a charm!" We hear the refrain "They don't make 'em like they used to" because, well, they really don't make 'em like they used to.

For brands in a post-Amazon world, the goal isn't just about rediscovering the quality of a bygone era. It's about inventing a new product altogether.

Look at what's happening in industries beyond retail. In transportation, up-and-coming brands such as Uber, which is less than six years old and valued at $17 billion,[18] prove that even the most established industries can be transformed by providing a better—often *much* better—experience. Airbnb, valued at $10 billion,[19] has done the same for the hotel industry. Both Uber and Airbnb have successfully challenged the value of a costly taxi medallion or a room at the Holiday Inn, respectively, when an affordable, on-demand ride home in someone else's car or a decent, low-cost bed will do.[20] Uber and Airbnb exist for one reason alone: their focus on what customers want and how to deliver it in the best way possible while eliminating excess cost is nothing short of an obsession. To them, nothing else matters.

We're now seeing a similar mindset disrupt retail. From the 1970s through the end of the century, consumers cared a lot about choice and assortment, and they were willing to tolerate whatever combination of brands, quality, and price was available at the local mall. Today, consumers know they can buy the same products online from multiple retailers around the world. As technology evolves, consumers can have their cake and eat it, too. They can buy any product they want at the best price available at midnight or at noon. They can build real relationships with brands that treat them like individuals, stand for something, and deliver great products.

The Power of Transparency

Young brands have a distinct advantage over traditional retailers: their customers are fiercely loyal. Why? Because they have taken the capital that technology has freed up and redeployed it toward products and services that most benefit their customers.

To explain what we mean by that, we'll use American Giant—the company with which we, this book's authors, are both most familiar (full disclosure: one of us founded the company).

For American Giant, making clothes in the United States is vitally important. The company values the creation of skilled jobs at a time of intense handwringing over the death of manufacturing jobs at home. Early on, company leaders decided to put American Giant's primary production in the heartland of what was once the country's top apparel-producing region: North and South Carolina. Yes, the overall manufacturing costs for American Giant exceed those of virtually all clothing brands that make their products overseas. But the company knows that its customers value high-quality, affordable goods made in the United States.

American Giant invests in US manufacturing because it can, profitably. The company does not have a huge infrastructure of stores, suppliers, and inventory to support—and it spends virtually nothing on marketing. It's making a bet that, if it delivers a product built according to values that customers support (for example, American jobs), customers will spread the word virally through their social networks. With that level of exposure, customers don't need physical stores and American Giant doesn't need expensive marketing campaigns. American Giant customers have responded in droves.

There is another factor defining retail's future: transparency. Thanks in large part to the Internet

Examples of this new generation of retailer abound. Some create a direct bond with their customers through brand values. Some focus on experience. Others rely on assortment, and still others distinguish themselves through quality. The best do all four.

bullhorn, consumers today know what's happening behind the scenes at many companies, not just retailers, and they're holding these companies accountable. Paying lip service to ethical labor practices or cleaner manufacturing processes won't work anymore. When brands talk about the values they stand for, they have to mean it. And they have to deliver on it.

This basic idea—of eliminating needless costs and redeploying the liberated capital in ways that matter most to consumers—is at the heart of all humanizers. Examples of this new generation of retailer abound. Some create a direct bond with their customers through brand values. Some focus on experience. Others rely on assortment, and still others distinguish themselves through quality. The best do all four. Whether they ultimately succeed or fail doesn't matter as much as the legacy they leave behind: an entirely new model for delivering what customers want *and* inviting those same customers to participate actively in the process of creating and making what they want.

The takeaway? Business today really *is* personal.

More Than Lip Service

Just about every brand tries to sell customers on the ideas of love, delight, and experience. Aside from notable exceptions, few brands truly deliver on these concepts, because they're trapped by the confines of the traditional retail model.

Many brands—distracted by the challenges of managing large real estate and marketing operations—will respond to the new paradigm in one of two ways. They will avoid developing real relationships with their customers and what they care about—whether it's the type of ingredients used, the manufacturing locale, or the carbon footprint left behind. That's the easy way out. The second response will be to fake it. They will embrace products and services that do little more than automate and streamline humanity. Already bots on Twitter auto-respond to complaints. Form emails from donotreply@domainname.com only make the problem worse. Name a customer who wants to receive this response to a complaint or question: "As a valued customer, we value your valuable concerns and input. Because we value you so much, we'll respond to your valuable inquiry within the next 48 hours."

Hollow words like these don't work. In today's world of transparency, brands can't pretend. They can't lie. Customers have incredible visibility, and they share what they know *instantly*.

Customer Backlash: Two Case Studies

Ask PepsiCo. In 2013, the maker of Gatorade said it would eliminate a controversial ingredient —brominated vegetable oil—from the popular sports drink after an online petition started by a 15-year-old girl calling for its removal went viral.[21] Nearly overnight PepsiCo found itself scrambling to contain a rapidly growing crisis.

Then there's Lululemon Athletica. Lululemon spent years cultivating one of the most beloved brands in apparel. Built from a simple concept of a great-fitting, high-quality yoga pant, Lululemon became the go-to pants for women whether they did downward dogs or not. Today, customers and critics are questioning the company's commitment to high quality since they learned that a line of yoga pants made in China were noticeably transparent when worn. The incident only fueled doubts about Lululemon's once-stellar trajectory,[22] and Lululemon's market cap has since fallen by about half as of this book's publication.

The lesson: simply declaring your devotion to customers, a value, or a cause won't do. You have to live by that devotion. We exist at a time when customers, even a teenager, can change the way a multimillion-dollar product is made and sold— simply by speaking up. Commitments to customers and their values have to be genuine.

In the end, post-Amazon brands won't compete on scale or optimization. They will compete and succeed on customer experience, devotion, and lasting relationships grounded in trust. They will win by changing the orientation of their business and by making the customer, as the saying goes, their "true north." ■

XT

WHAT'S NEXT—FOR AMAZON AND EVERYBODY ELSE

In the post-Amazon world, not all brands will
die, but every one of them will change. They have no
choice. To understand who wins and who loses, let's
take a closer look at the primary ways companies
seek to differentiate themselves today.

For commodity products, such as paper towels
and laundry detergent, price and convenience will
often matter to the exclusion of all else. The same
holds true for commodity-type clothing such as
diapers and undershirts. But as we move up the scale
to experience, or the feeling of excitement that a
brand generates, things get interesting.

The new drivers of love are brand and quality
(see graphic on page 51)—the new imperatives for
great retailers going forward. In the old world,
you could build a brand with money, operational
efficiency, and real estate. In the new world, that
playbook doesn't work.

Don't get us wrong: we applaud operational
efficiency. Exceptional companies like Amazon,
Walmart, Zara, and Uniqlo will continue to thrive,
because they excel at delivering quality products at
great prices and in the most convenient ways possible
for customers. But in a world where efficient supply
chains and logistics become ubiquitous, every retail
brand will operate efficiently. Retailers will be forced
to tighten every aspect of their business, cutting all
excess. They will rely on social media for demand
aggregation, software for real-time pricing, the Web
for shopping, and robots for shipping packages.
Automation ultimately will commoditize what today
look like competitive advantages.

In the end, the rise of Walmart and Amazon
marks the triumph of automation. Post-Amazon
retailers represent the return to humanization in
customer-brand relationships.

New Virtuous Cycle: Lessons from Amazon

For humanizers, growth takes a backseat to a
loftier goal: creating more dynamic, thoughtful,

and personalized experiences for customers. We've talked a lot about these ideas in previous chapters. Massive efficiencies in distribution and marketing enabled by connected, mobile, and participatory consumers free companies to do what human beings do best: generate new ideas and engage with other human beings through real relationships. The strategy isn't to deploy technology as a means to automate as much of the retail experience as possible, but to leverage it to generate real love for a product, service, or brand.

That's the new virtuous cycle in the post-Amazon world, and it's based on intangibles that retailers can't automate. They can only feed, nurture, and grow them.

Jeff Bezos is unapologetically zealous about the virtuous cycle he famously created for Amazon (see graphic on page 52). The Bezos cycle invests in customer loyalty by getting prices as low as possible. Here's how Brad Stone, senior writer at *Bloomberg Businessweek*, describes this cycle in his book *The Everything Store: Jeff Bezos and the Age of Amazon*:

> [L]ower prices led to more customer visits. More customers increased the volume of sales and attracted more commission-paying third-party sellers to the site. That allowed Amazon to get more out of fixed costs like the fulfillment centers and the servers needed to run the website. This greater efficiency then enabled it to lower prices further. Feed any part of this flywheel, they reasoned, and it should accelerate the loop.

The focus for Bezos has always been on making things easy for consumers and keeping prices low in order to build loyalty. His ability to master the science of automation to deliver on that focus takes your breath away. Bezos's focus on customers is fanatical. But the core problem he's solving for them

THE DRIVERS OF LOVE

As customers increasingly expect the optimization of price and convenience, they are beginning to seek out the elements that they love.

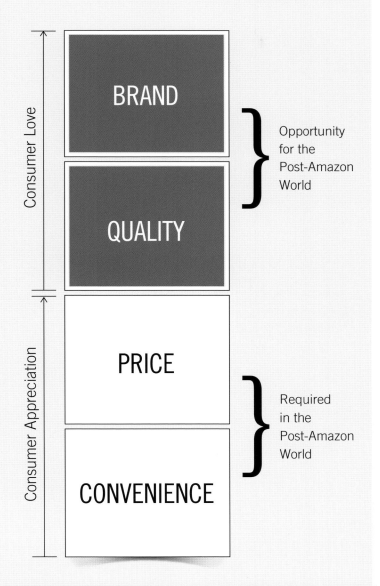

AMAZON AND BIG BOX RETAIL PUT GROWTH IN THE CENTER

The classic cycle used by Amazon as the model for everything it did: The heart of the model is scale, and the means to reach it is lower prices.

POST-AMAZON-WORLD COMPANIES PUT LOVE AT THEIR CORE

Post-Amazon companies put customer love at the center to unlock passion and loyalty from their customers to further amplify and accelerate the brand.

differs fundamentally from what drives the new breed of retailer. Whereas Bezos obsesses about how to sell commodity products to customers at the lowest prices and as efficiently as possible, the next-generation retailers seek an entirely different kind of relationship with customers.

In this new relationship, consumers help shape production schedules. They share products that they love and let the world know about the ones they don't. They drive both innovation and marketing. In turn, new brands rely on technology to streamline those interactions. They build businesses—and products—that are free of old cost structures and are heavily engaged in social media. In this model, the brands' ultimate goal is to create lasting customer relationships, and they know consumers will hold them accountable for any broken promises. The new world makes it possible for brands to have relationships with customers that are one-on-one and built to last.

Post-Amazon retailers achieve the best innovation by focusing on products consumers want and avoiding products they don't. They focus on developing personalized relationships between brands and people at a scale sufficient to meet customer demand.

In this new landscape, companies like Lolly Wolly Doodle and American Giant create a new virtuous cycle, which assumes easy access online. The cycle also assumes the brand has rejected the old cost structure in favor of investments in products and experiences. In this world, size alone doesn't matter. Successful retailers can be multibillion-dollar operations or they can be mom-and-pop shops catering to a select audience. Scale is no longer the end goal; it happens only to satisfy demand.

Great products generate great word of mouth. Great word of mouth spreads through social media. Fast response to consumer participation through social media leads to even greater products. And then the cycle repeats and continues to be reinforced and supported by the core values of the brand.

Over time, post-Amazon brands build love, loyalty, and lasting relationships that can't be easily displaced. Why? Because they exist based on true values, real experiences, and genuine creativity, none of which can be automated. These companies set an uncharted pace for—and efficiency in—building a brand while doing so at a fraction of the cost of any companies in the history of retail.

Winners and Losers in the Post-Amazon Retail World

Ultimately, the core elements—namely, operational efficiencies such as assortment, price, and access—that once defined success in brick-and-mortar stores are becoming irrelevant. An entirely new hierarchy of needs has started to emerge.

In this new world, great legacy brands like Levi's and Polo will do very well if they make the transition to the digital world. They are classic icons of American style and will benefit from the goodwill they've built with customers. But to succeed long-term, these legacy brands can no longer rely on other retailers to sell their products. They have to learn how to leverage technology to create direct relationships with their customers online.

What about the rest of old-world retail—the Hollisters, Quiksilvers, and Foot Lockers that make up a sea of vendors at the local mall? For these traditional brands, which are stuck in what we call the "mushy middle," a frightening future looms. Look past the logos and you'll find they are merely managers of vast real estate and marketing operations. None of them are in the business of selling what consumers actually want. If top-line growth continues to fade, they will suffocate under their own weight. Recall what Howard Schultz of Starbucks suggested about retail's giant ecosystem: coffee shops and food courts alike pay the price for declining foot traffic at the mall.

Now may be the most exciting time to be in retail. But for retailers caught in the mushy middle, it's one of the scariest.

Emotional Plus Rational Connections

The main advantage in a post-Amazon world goes to young retailers. They can start fresh, unburdened by the distribution and marketing models that shackle old-line retail. This freedom gives them the extra capital to build the rational and emotional connections with consumers that all brands will need in order to thrive.

What are "emotional" and "rational" connections? Emotional connections are about the story of a company, its community of customers, and the richness of its media. Rational connections, on the other hand, involve how well companies deliver on what they promise, whether that means price, point of view, experience, or quality.

American Giant builds real and rational connections with customers through good products, fair prices, and excellent customer service. The company creates an emotional bond with customers through a value system centered on a commitment to American-made products and a "Don't get comfortable" motto that creates purpose and soul for its clothing and for customers.

Brands have always been about connecting emotionally with people. Great brands in any era have done this well. Some, such as Levi's, have done it for more than 100 years. Some have done it for a far shorter time. But at their heart lies the idea of connecting emotionally with people.

Emerging retailers looking to create emotional and rational connections with consumers benefit from several trends, first discussed in Chapter

Two, that didn't exist in e-commerce's earlier wave of disruption:

- Consumers are moving online in droves.

- Adoption of mobile technology is increasing online shopping.

- Mining of big data is driving better customer experiences.

- Social media is changing the dynamic of brand building.

These factors create a new dynamic. Rather than choose to focus solely on the low-level needs, such as access, price, and operational efficiency, or on emotional items, such as values and soul, new brands can focus on both. They can zero in on the things that make great brands great: emotional and rational connections, all happening at once.

Now it's no longer sufficient for brands to deliver an emotional connection without a great product or a great product without an emotional connection. They need both. Thanks to technology, brands can deliver both in ways they never could before. ■

POST-AMAZON COMPANIES ARE LIBERATED TO EXECUTE ON ALL FRONTS LIKE NEVER BEFORE

Enabled by technology, post-Amazon companies can drive great operational efficiency while focusing on delivering what the customer truly cares about.

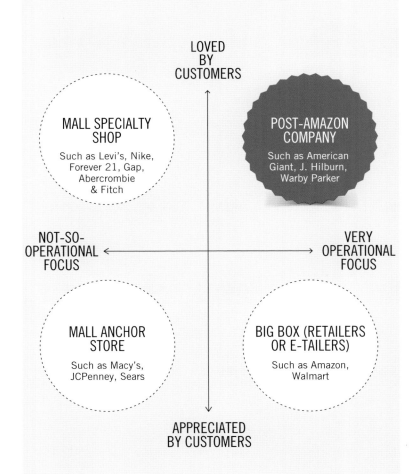

LOVED BY CUSTOMERS

MALL SPECIALTY SHOP

Such as Levi's, Nike, Forever 21, Gap, Abercrombie & Fitch

POST-AMAZON COMPANY

Such as American Giant, J. Hilburn, Warby Parker

NOT-SO-OPERATIONAL FOCUS

VERY OPERATIONAL FOCUS

MALL ANCHOR STORE

Such as Macy's, JCPenney, Sears

BIG BOX (RETAILERS OR E-TAILERS)

Such as Amazon, Walmart

APPRECIATED BY CUSTOMERS

CHAPTER FIVE

GO

THE FREEDOM TO "GROW GOOD"

We've established that consumers value efficiency, quality, low prices, and the human touch in their interactions with brands today. And we've explained how the Internet megaphone holds brands accountable and puts a premium on transparency. But there's another important aspect of changing consumer behavior—and it's a critical piece of the post-Amazon puzzle.

New brands have not only the financial resources to *do* more for the customer, because of a more efficient cost structure, but also the opportunity to *be* more for the customer. This dynamic is important because consumers care more than ever about the good a company is doing. These goals are possible because humanizers have the economic freedom to define clear values and build them into the DNA of their businesses. These values reflect a sensibility that is as important to the business and its leaders as are the products they sell and the people they hire.

A commitment to values follows an arc similar to the one that has reshaped the way customers engage with brands. Just as the quality of customer service has boomeranged from highly personal at the mom-and-pop shop to clinically efficient at big box e-tailer and back to deeply intimate (often at scale) among post-Amazon brands, values no longer center on scale but instead on the canons that once defined the relationship between a customer and the corner store. Today, emerging brands value a new imperative: Be good. Do good. Or, as we like to say, "grow good."

For humanizers, crafting a set of brand values from day one and executing against them consistently aren't viewed as burdens, either financially or administratively. Rather, values are seen as an incredible opportunity to cement real, lasting relationships with consumers who share similar values. In this scenario, the more good a brand does, the more loyal customers become.

In the end, there is a spiral of life that gets created—and perpetuated.

Millennials: Paying Attention and Supporting Social Causes

Doing good is especially important to millennial consumers. Survey after survey reveals that millennials, who make up the bulk of shoppers moving online and represent $200 billion in annual buying power, are the most socially conscious generation we have ever seen. Eighty-seven percent of millennials donated to a nonprofit organization in 2013, according to the 2014 Millennial Impact Report.[23] But that's not all. They are also voting with their wallets. A 2011 study found that one of every three young consumers (ages 20 to 35) will boycott or support a business based on his or her interest in particular causes.[24] More compelling evidence came out of the 2012 Millennial Impact Report: [25]

- **More than 85 percent of millennials correlate their purchasing decisions and their willingness to recommend a brand to the social good a company is doing.**

- **When shopping, 86 percent of millennials want to learn about the relevant environmental issues from the brand itself.**

- **If the price and quality of a product are comparable, millennials are likely to switch brands if one is committed to a good cause.**

For traditional brick-and-mortar brands, this social activism poses some serious challenges. Even if these brands genuinely want to "do good," they most likely can't afford to. A cottage industry has grown up around the notion of corporate social responsibility as evidence grows that consumers seek out businesses committed to social causes and, likewise, boycott businesses that appear to violate

> New brands have not only the financial resources to *do* more for the customer, because of a more efficient cost structure, but also the opportunity to *be* more for the customer.

their personal ethos. But don't be fooled; many of the so-called social good initiatives you see and hear about come directly out of a company's marketing budget. These efforts reflect more "good washing" than actual good doing.

True in Name and in Practice

To succeed, retail brands today must inspire love, and it has to be real. For consumers to pick up a retailer's banner and spread the word, they have to believe in what the company creates, what it stands for, or both. When customers believe, they will eagerly pick up the brand's bullhorn—and, thanks to technology, they will do it at light speed.

Select brands have long understood the power of values. Patagonia, for instance, has a strong reputation for its commitment to corporate values. For decades, the company has donated 1 percent of sales to environmental protection efforts. It funds documentaries about climate change and makes it easy to recycle clothes. Patagonia's founder embraces an ethos first articulated by a celebrated ad executive in the late 1960s: A principle is not a principle until it costs you something.[26]

Customers don't buy Patagonia's products because they're looking for bargains. They know they can buy quality outdoor gear for roughly the same price at much larger retailers such as Columbia Sportswear. Patagonia's customers remain loyal because they believe in the values of the brand.

TOMS Shoes serves as another poster child for company values beloved by customers. The Los Angeles–based company started out selling espadrilles, which is arguably the most basic, seemingly unimaginative shoe this side of a sandal. And yet, TOMS footwear took the world by storm.

TOMS wants to make the world a better place, one pair of shoes at a time. To that end, for every pair of espadrilles sold, TOMS donates a pair to charity. It also provides eye care and clean water to impoverished children in dozens of countries. For TOMS, business is about helping people. Selling stylish shoes—and, more recently, eyewear and coffee—seems like an afterthought.

Then there's Chipotle Mexican Grill. The giant fast-food chain has capitalized on growing awareness of healthy organic food by releasing a series of video satires critical of industrial farming. The videos, which use humor to highlight the highly mechanized, disconnected relationship between people and the animals that sustain us, have been a huge hit on YouTube. The first, titled *The Scarecrow*, had garnered 13.5 million views in the 12 months since its September 2013 release. Chipotle lives by its motto—"Food with Integrity"—and is a darling of hungry consumers because of it.

For its part, American Giant believes that building a business that also generates skilled jobs offers customers real value. It works on the belief that, given the choice between higher quality at affordable prices and lower quality at lower prices, consumers will feel inspired to choose the label "Made in the USA." The value of at-home manufacturing is coded into the company's DNA.

Patagonia, TOMS, Chipotle, and American Giant marshal their values to engender love and loyalty. They sell their value system in the same way that Apple sells creativity and Nike sells athleticism. The difference, however, is that values aren't marketing ploys. They are real. And when a brand's values don't conform to communal values, the brand hears about it—at full volume.

The values a brand espouses have to make sense. They can't take a craven look at the causes people care about and then work backward from there. No one doubts that TOMS cares a great deal about the children to whom it donates shoes, or that Patagonia is truly devoted to protecting the environment where its customers live and play. But what if a maker of blue jeans decided to donate a share of profits to animal shelters? Sure, lots of people care about the overpopulation of dogs and cats, but the cause doesn't make sense for a brand that has nothing to do with domestic pets. Consumers would smell the falseness of it.

Real human values must coexist with sales in a post-Amazon world. Truly caring can mean creating manufacturing jobs in local communities. Or it can mean using only the best ingredients for your food and providing transparency to the customer. In short, new brands act more like people who care than businesses that sell.

Good Values Equals Good Business

Much of this book is about having your cake and eating it, too. By that we mean brands today can combine automation and a human touch to create amazing products at great prices. The post-Amazon world enables consumers and brands alike to do more than they ever imagined possible. The same dynamic applies to values. Modern business leaders don't have to embrace values out of the goodness of their hearts. They can embrace values because it's

Much of this book is about having your cake and eating it, too. By that we mean brands today can combine automation and a human touch to create amazing products at great prices.

smart business. Just as mall brands struggle with the spiral of death, new brands can benefit from a spiral of life that creates stronger and stronger bonds between brands and consumers.

We've written this book because brands are entering the most disruptive time in their history. This isn't hyperbole. Until now, every massive transformation in retail has represented the next logical step as new technological tools have become available, starting with the Sears Roebuck catalog and culminating in the rise of Amazon. What we're seeing today is different. Today, a brand can skyrocket to success almost overnight, not because it has the fastest checkout process or the savviest email marketing, but because it has discovered an entirely new model for retail. In this model, it can successfully combine the best of technology with a soul and make money at the same time.

Our message to young brands really is a simple one: Make great products. Stand for something. Build customer loyalty. Create an international brand at light speed. Never in the history of retail has the opportunity to build a brand been better. ∎

NOTES

1. Marshall Hargrave, "Searching for Value in a Beaten-Down Industry," The Motley Fool, July 15, 2004, http://www.fool.com/investing/general/2014/07/15/searching -for-value-in-a-beaten-down-industry.aspx; Hollie Shaw, "How American Apparel Fell into 'Dangerous Trap' of Retail Expansion Hype," *Financial Post*, July 12, 2014, http:// business.financialpost.com/2014/07/12/how-american-apparel-fell-into-dangerous -trap-of-retail-expansion-hype; "Will New Brand President Make a Difference for Abercrombie & Fitch?," *Forbes.com*, July 10, 2014, http://www.forbes.com/sites/ greatspeculations/2014/07/10/will-new-brand-president-make-a-difference-for -abercrombie-fitch; Lindsey Rupp, "Modesty Is the New Abercrombie," *Bloomberg Businessweek*, May 22, 2014, http://www.businessweek.com/articles/2014-05-22/ abercrombie-and-fitch-tries-to-win-teens-back-from-online-retail; Dana Mattioli, "Wet Seal Fires CEO as Financial Picture Weakens," *Wall Street Journal*, July 23, 2012, http://online.wsj.com/news/articles/SB10000872396390443437504577545202454192994; Phil Wahba, "Is Gap Stumbling Again?" *Fortune.com*, July 10, 2014, http://fortune .com/2014/07/10/gap-comparable-sales; David Hernandez, "Macy's Online Growth Masking Fundamental Problem," Seeking Alpha, July 10, 2014, http://seekingalpha .com/article/2308655-macys-online-growth-masking-fundamental-problem; Fletcher Greer, "JCPenney: Don't Try to Catch a Falling Star," Seeking Alpha, May 23, 2014, http://seekingalpha.com/article/2235123-j-c-penney-dont-try-to-catch-a-falling-star; and Justin Lahart, "Sears Catalog of Worry Isn't Getting Thinner," *Wall Street Journal*, May 22, 2014, http://online.wsj.com/news/articles/SB10001424052702303749904579578 3383365124424.

2. Anupreeta Das, "Buffett's Achilles Heel: Investing in Retail," *Wall Street Journal*, July 17, 2014, http://online.wsj.com/articles/buffetts-achilles-heel-retail-investing -1405539148.

3. E-commerce sales in the United States grew 6.4 percent in the second quarter of 2014, according to government data. *U.S. Census Bureau News*, August 15, 2014, http:// www.census.gov/retail/mrts/www/data/pdf/ec_current.pdf. Also, eMarketer predicted that US retail sales would grow 45 percent, to $440.4 billion, between 2014 and 2017. "Total US Retail Sales Top $4.5 Trillion in 2013, Outpace GDP Growth," eMarketer, April 10, 2014, http://www.emarketer.com/Article/Total-US-Retail-Sales-Top-3645 -Trillion-2013-Outpace-GDP-Growth/1010756.

4. Shelly Banjo, "Slowing Customer Traffic Worries U.S. Retailers," *Wall Street Journal*, July 10, 2014, http://online.wsj.com/articles/promotions-drive-sales-for-retailers-in -june-1404998141; and Douglas A. McIntyre, "Thousands of Major Retailer Locations Could Close This Year," *24/7WallSt.com*, May 23, 2014, http://247wallst.com/ retail/2014/05/23/thousands-of-major-retailer-locations-could-close-this-year.

5. "Starbucks Reports Record Q1 Results and Reaffirms FY14 Growth Targets," Starbucks Corporation, January 23, 2014, http://investor.starbucks.com/phoenix .zhtml?c=99518&p=irol-newsArticle&ID=1893168&highlight=.

6. Venessa Wong, "Why Starbucks Worries about Retailers' Dwindling Foot Traffic," *Bloomberg Businessweek*, January 24, 2014, http://www.businessweek.com/ articles/2014-01-24/why-starbucks-worries-about-retailers-dwindling-foot-traffic.

7. Don Reisinger, "Circuit City: A Eulogy," CNET, January 16, 2009, http://www.cnet .com/news/circuit-city-a-eulogy; "Best Buy's Decline Not Complete," Seeking Alpha, July 13, 2014, http://seekingalpha.com/article/2312055-best-buys-decline-not -complete; Phil Wahba, "PetSmart Now in Activist's Crosshairs after Years of Ignoring Amazon, Wal-Mart," *Fortune.com*, July 3, 2014, http://fortune.com/2014/07/03/ petsmart-jana-partners; and Elizabeth A. Harris, "RadioShack in Need of Rewiring," *New York Times*, August 19, 2014, http://www.nytimes.com/2014/08/20/business/ a-supplier-to-tinkerers-radioshack-struggles-in-a-wireless-world.html?_r=0.

8. Ad Age Research Report: Retail Marketing, *Advertising Age*, September 30, 2013, gaia .adage.com/images/bin/pdf/kantarretailmarketing093013.pdf.

9. Sam Ro, "Here Are the Profit Margins for Every Sector in the S&P 500," *Business Insider*, August 16, 2012, http://www.businessinsider.com/sector-profit-margins -sp-500-2012-8.

10. Rick Aristotle Munarriz, "Can Turnarounds Save JCPenney, Sears and Best Buy?," Daily Finance, May 29, 2014, http://www. dailyfinance.com/2014/05/29/retail -turnarounds-jcpenney-sears-best-buy.

11. Barbara Farfan, "All Retail Store Closings—US Retail Industry Chains to Close Stores," About.com, accessed October 1, 2014, http://retailindustry.about.com/od/ USRetailStoreClosingInfoFAQs/fl/All-2014-Store-Closings-US-Retail-Industry -Chains-to-Close-Stores.htm.

12. Tom Foster, "The Startup That Conquered Facebook Sales," *Inc. Magazine*, June 2014, http://www.inc.com/magazine/201406/tom-foster/lolly-wolly-doodle-explosive-growth -from-facebook-sales.html.

13 Shibani Mahtani, "Apparel Retailer Gap Forges Ahead in Myanmar," *WSJ.com*, June 6, 2014, http://online.wsj.com/articles/apparel-retailer-gap-forges-ahead-in-myanmar -1402091240.

14. Susan Berfield and Manuel Baigorri, "Zara's Fast-Fashion Edge," *Bloomberg Businessweek*, November 14, 2013, http://www.businessweek.com/articles/2013 -11-14/2014-outlook-zaras-fashion-supply-chain-edge; and Megan Durisin, "How Clothing Chain Uniqlo Is Taking Over the World," *Business Insider*, April 26, 2013, http://www.businessinsider.com/the-story-of-uniqlo-2013-4?op=1.

15. Nicholas Carlson, "Warby Parker Wants to Destroy a $20 Billion Company That Charges Customers Insane Prices," *Business Insider*, December 23, 2012, http://www .businessinsider.com/this-startup-wants-to-destroy-a-20-billion-company-that-rips-off -its-customers-2012-12?op=1.

16. Editors of *Inc.,* "The 2012 Inc. 5000 List," http://www.inc.com/inc5000/list/2012.

17. Farhad Manjoo, "This Is the Greatest Hoodie Ever Made," *Slate.com,* December 4, 2012, http://www.slate.com/articles/technology/technology/2012/12/american_giant _hoodie_this_is_the_greatest_sweatshirt_known_to_man.html.

18. Serena Saitto and Brad Stone, "Uber Sets Valuation Record of $17 Billion in New Funding," Bloomberg.com, June 7, 2014, http://www.bloomberg.com/news/2014-06-06/ uber-sets-valuation-record-of-17-billion-in-new-funding.html.

19. Michael J. De La Merced, "Airbnb Said to Close Fund-Raising Deal with Group Led by TPG," *NYTimes.com*, April 18, 2014, http://dealbook.nytimes.com/2014/04/18/ airbnb-said-to-close-fund-raising-deal-with-group-led-by-tpg.

20. Evidence is growing that car-sharing services like Uber and Lyft are disrupting ground transportation as we know it—and fast. In San Francisco alone, the number of taxi rides plunged 65 percent between March 2013 and July 2014, *San Francisco Chronicle* staff reported. Michael Cabanatuan, "Ride Services Decimate S.F.'s Taxi Industry's Business," *SFGate.com*, September 16, 2014, http://www.sfgate.com/ bayarea/article/Taxi-use-plummets-in-San-Francisco-65-percent-in-5760251 .php?utm_source=nextdraft&utm_medium=email.

21. Stephanie Strom, "PepsiCo Will Halt Use of Additive in Gatorade," *NYTimes.com,* January 25, 2013, http://dinersjournal.blogs.nytimes.com/2013/01/25/gatorade-listens -to-a-teen-and-changes-its-formula/?_php=true&_type=blogs&_r=0.

22. Michael Carter, "What Really Happened to Lululemon?," The Motley Fool, July 15, 2014, http://www.fool.com/investing/general/2014/07/15/what-really-happened-to -lululemon.aspx.

23. The 2014 Millennial Impact Report, Achieve and Johnson Grossnickle and Associates, 2014, www.themillennialimpact.com/2014-research.

24. "The Future of Social Activism," TBWA\Worldwide, accessed September 30, 2014, http://www.tbwa.com/search/future-of%20social%20activism.

25. The 2012 Millennial Impact Report, Achieve and Johnson Grossnickle and Associates, 2012, www.themillennialimpact.com/research-2012.

26. Several sources attribute the saying to Bill Bernach, cofounder of what is now known as DDB Worldwide, a global ad agency owned by Omnicom Group. See, for example, "A Principle Isn't a Principle Until It Costs You Something," *Huffington Post,* October 4, 2011, http://www.huffingtonpost.com/mark-a-obrien/advertising-agencies -intellectual-property_b_994091.html.

ABOUT THE AUTHORS

Bayard Winthrop
Bayard founded American Giant after spending nearly 20 years running businesses in the consumer products space. He began his career in corporate finance at Donaldson, Lufkin & Jenrette, but soon he left investment banking for a career as a business leader and innovator. He has held key leadership positions at a variety of brands, including Atlas Snow-Shoe (eventually sold to K2 Sports), WebChat Broadcasting System (sold to Disney), Freebord Manufacturing (privately held), and Chrome Industries (privately held).

Randy Komisar

Randy Komisar is a general partner at Kleiner Perkins Caufield & Byers, a venture capital firm that invests in disruptive entrepreneurs looking to create and build world-changing businesses.

Earlier in his career, he was co-founder of computer software company Claris Corp., served as CEO for both LucasArts Entertainment and Crystal Dynamics, and acted as a "virtual CEO" for such companies as WebTV and GlobalGiving. Randy also served as CFO of GO Corp. and as senior counsel for Apple Computer following a private practice in technology law.

Randy is the author of critically acclaimed, best-selling books *The Monk and the Riddle* and *Getting to Plan B,* in which he covers topics such as personal improvement, business management and innovation. He is also a frequent lecturer and writer on topics such as leadership and entrepreneurship at academic institutions and in publications in the US and abroad. Randy holds a B.A. in economics from Brown University and a J.D. from Harvard Law School.